EVERY CHILD'S BOOK
OF
NURSERY SONGS

Our book is affectionately dedicated
to
MATTHEW BLYTON
CORIN BUCKERIDGE
and
MARCUS DU SAUTOY

EVERY CHILD'S BOOK
OF
NURSERY SONGS

Selected by
DONALD MITCHELL

Arranged by
CAREY BLYTON

Illustrated by
ALAN HOWARD

CROWN PUBLISHERS, INC. • NEW YORK

Published in the United States by Crown Publishers, Inc.,
One Park Avenue, New York, New York 10016

Published in Great Britain by Faber and Faber Limited,
3 Queen Square, London WC1N 3AU

Manufactured in Great Britain

Originally published in Great Britain under the title
The Faber Book of Nursery Songs by Faber and Faber Limited

Library of Congress Cataloging in Publication Data
Main entry under title:
Every child's book of nursery songs.
With piano acc.
Originally published: The Faber book of nursery
songs. London: Faber, 1968.
Summary: An illustrated collection of ninety-one
nursery rhymes set to music.
1. Children's Songs.   2. Kindergarten—Music.
3. Nursery schools—Music.   4. Nursery rhymes—
Musical settings. [1. Nursery rhymes. 2. Songs]
I. Mitchell, Donald, 1925-   .   II. Blyton, Carey.
III. Howard, Alan, ill.   IV. Faber book of nursery songs.
[M1990.E94 1984]   84-759337
ISBN 0-517-55677-4
10 9 8 7 6 5 4 3 2 1
First 1985 Edition

CONTENTS

CONTENTS

INTRODUCTION

FROM the flood of traditional works in England and other countries, a steady stream of musical literature for children has flowed into the New World. In the best tradition of early collectors, a net has been cast wide by the English editors of EVERY CHILD'S BOOK OF NURSERY SONGS—an outstanding selection of nursery rhymes, melodies, and songs that past generations have known and sung.

This lilting collection is arranged and prepared with a fresh approach that adds vigor to its use in homes and nursery schools, kindergartens, and primary grades of America. Donald Mitchell selected the songs and Carey Blyton made the arrangements for them. Both are outstanding musicologists, well known in the United States as well as in England. They point out that it is always a desperate business, when preparing a collection, to decide what to omit and what to include. Everyone has his own favorite, and the editors hope they have included so many favorites that everyone or almost everyone will be happy about the selections. They have also included some fresh and little-known songs that will become favorites of many people. Also, they believe that this book sustains a common musical heritage along with an aim to serve the modern child.

To this end, best-loved Mother Goose verses and other rhymes, and popular as well as unfamiliar melodies, have been carefully selected from a variety of versions. There are no exotic accompaniments. Instead, simple piano arrangements accompany the tuneful, jaunty rhymes. Wherever possible, this musical anthology has "included suggestions for the use of percussion instruments . . ." and other devices that foster classroom participation.

The absence of intricate accompaniment not only enhances the listening and singing properties of the nursery songs but also makes it possible for teachers and parents to pick out tunes on the piano without difficulty. Spurred by the tidy arrangements of musical notes, the adult may want to implement each score by adding chords, or by letting the children use bells, triangles, cymbals, or even drums.

The vibrant illustrations are in rhythmic and enchantingly childlike agreement with the verses and the music they interpret. Their strong colors and

INTRODUCTION

designs give another dimension of pleasure to a collection in which every effort has been made to retain the authentic form of the verses, and to accommodate them so that as far as possible they exactly fit the tunes as well as the times and the young audiences. But let's let Donald Mitchell and Carey Blyton have their final say about the texts.

"We have included, to the best of our knowledge, the full texts in, we hope, their authentic form. In a few cases, it will be found that the second (or subsequent) verses do not exactly fit the tune. In general, it is absolutely clear how these, for the most part, extra (or missing) syllables should be musically accommodated or adjusted, and we are content to leave such variations to the natural musical sense of our performers. It would have been needlessly pedantic and confusing, we felt, to notate these minor variants. In even fewer cases, it may be found that the second (or subsequent) verses or lines don't fit the music at all. No matter. It seemed a pity to exclude the words—which in themselves were often of much charm—on purely musical grounds. We suggest that when the music, so to say, runs out, our performers should stop and read the rest. And of course, as sometimes happens, when one tune serves more than one text, we have not hesitated to use the tune more than once."

High praise goes to the editor and the arranger who have compiled this collection by sifting the gold from the dross so that an outstanding collection of musical treasure can now be transmitted in a delightful way to a modern generation in America.

BERNICE CULLINAN, PH.D.
Specialist in children's books and music, New York University

CONSTANTINE GEORGIOU, PH.D.
Specialist in children's literature, New York University

A NOTE ON THE MUSIC

The arrangements of these tunes have been kept as simple as possible, and they are intended for use by either non-specialist teachers or mothers or other relatives whose piano technique is limited. The tunes are in the right hand and the accompaniments lie *entirely* beneath the left hand in the majority of cases.

It will be seen that several accompanimental patterns, both harmonic and rhythmic, have been used a number of times. This is not due to a paucity of invention on the part of the arranger, but is, rather, a deliberate attempt to assist the generally over-worked teacher: once an accompanimental pattern has been learned it will serve—with the slight variations shown—for quite a number of tunes, thus avoiding the necessity of learning a new accompaniment for each new tune.

Introductions and codettas are optional and, if desired, only the actual melody—which appears between the first and last double bar-lines, with any appropriate up-beat before the first—need be played; where required, shorter-version endings are given in brackets. If introductions and codettas are used, then once only—at the start and the end of a song—would suffice, though naturally they may be used for every verse if desired. Tempo and expression directions are only suggestions, and speeds in quicker tunes will depend upon the player's individual dexterity.

Most tunes have below them a part for speech or unpitched percussion (a single line or staff), or pitched percussion (a small treble clef stave). These parts are *purely optional* and *only suggestions*: the teacher may find them useful as they stand, or prefer to use them as a basis for something simpler or perhaps more elaborate. (See p. 10 for comments on percussion instruments in general and the spoken parts in particular.)

Occasionally, there is a suggestion for the use of some melodic instrument (marked M ̄ ̄ ̄ ̄), in which case recorder, harmonica,

A NOTE ON THE MUSIC

clarina, melodica or any other suitable instrument should be used if available. Here again, the use of these instruments is entirely optional.

Those tunes which are also rounds have been noted as such, and older children may like to try them in this way after the tunes have been learned in unison. A number of tunes, or parts of tunes, which are not normally considered to be rounds, but which in fact work as such, have also been noted.

SPOKEN PARTS:
These are invariably animal noises in the appropriate songs. The class should be divided into two groups, one group singing the song, with the other group providing the noises; the groups can interchange.

PERCUSSION INSTRUMENTS:
Unpitched: Bells, Castanets, Cymbals, Gong Drum, Maracas, Rhythm Sticks, Side Drum, Tambour, Tambourine, Triangle, etc.
Note: In the absence of any real instruments, the rhythms may be played on makeshift "instruments", e.g., pencils tapping on desks, hand-clapping, foot-tapping, etc.
Pitched: Chime Bars, Glockenspiel, Metallophone, Xylophone, etc.

Carey Blyton

Swanley, Kent
August, 1967

ACKNOWLEDGEMENT

We should like to express our indebtedness to two invaluable works by Iona and Peter Opie, *The Oxford Dictionary of Nursery Rhymes* (1951) and *The Oxford Nursery Rhyme Book* (1955), to which we have frequently turned for clarification and guidance.

D.M., C.B.

TURN AGAIN, WHITTINGTON*

Turn again, Whittington,
Thou worthy citizen,
Lord Mayor of London.

*This song may also be sung as a round for 3 voices, as indicated.

POLLY, PUT THE KETTLE ON

Polly, put the kettle on, Polly, put the kettle on, Polly put the kettle on: We'll all have tea. Sukey, take it off a-gain, Sukey, take it off a-gain, Sukey, take it off a-gain: They've all gone a-way.

Polly, put the kettle on

Polly, put the kettle on,
Polly, put the kettle on,
Polly, put the kettle on:
We'll all have tea.
Sukey, take it off again,
Sukey, take it off again,
Sukey, take it off again:
They've all gone away.

Bye, baby bunting,
Daddy's gone a-hunting,
Gone to get a rabbit skin,
To wrap the baby bunting in.

JACK SPRAT

Jack Sprat could eat no fat, His wife could eat no lean; And so be-tween them both, you see, They licked the plat-ter clean.

Jack Sprat could eat no fat,
His wife could eat no lean;
And so between them both, you see,
They licked the platter clean.

Gaily

1. Sim-ple Si-mon met a pie-man
Lu-cy Lock-et lost her pock-et,

Go - ing to the fair;— Says Sim-ple Si-mon to the pie-man,
Kit-ty Fish-er found it, 7 Not a pen-ny was there in it,

"Let me taste your ware".
On - ly rib -bon round it.

Lucy Locket

Lucy Locket lost her pocket,
Kitty Fisher found it,
Not a penny was there in it,
Only ribbon round it.

16

Simple Simon

Simple Simon met a pieman
Going to the fair;
Says Simple Simon to the pieman,
"Let me taste your ware".

Says the pieman to Simple Simon,
"Show me first your penny";
Says Simple Simon to the pieman,
"Indeed I have not any".

Simple Simon went a-fishing,
For to catch a whale;
All the water he had got
Was in his mother's pail.

Simple Simon went to look
If plums grew on a thistle;
He pricked his fingers very much,
Which made poor Simon whistle.

He went for water in a sieve
But soon it all fell through;
And now poor Simple Simon
Bids you all adieu.

Moderate tempo

1. Jack and Jill Went up the hill, To fetch a pail of wa-ter; Jack fell down, And broke his crown, And Jill came tum-bling af-ter.

*Although not usually sung as a round, this tune will in fact work as such. The asterisk shows the entry-point of the 2nd. voice.

Jack and Jill

Jack and Jill
Went up the hill,
To fetch a pail of water;
Jack fell down,
And broke his crown,
And Jill came tumbling after.

Then up Jack got,
And home did trot,
As fast as he could caper;
To old Dame Dob,
Who patched his nob
With vinegar and brown paper.

When Jill came in,
How she did grin
To see Jack's paper plaster;
Her mother, vexed,
Did whip her next,
For laughing at Jack's disaster.

Now Jack did laugh
And Jill did cry,
But her tears did soon abate;
Then Jill did say,
That they should play
At see-saw across the gate.

LONDON'S BURNING

*This song may also be sung as a round for 3 voices, as indicated.

London's burning

London's burning,
London's burning,
Fetch the engines,
Fetch the engines,
Fire! Fire!
Fire! Fire!
Pour on water, pour on water.

OLD MOTHER HUBBARD

Old Mother Hubbard
Went to the cupboard,
To fetch her poor dog a bone;
But when she got there
The cupboard was bare
And so the poor dog had none.

She went to the baker's
To buy him some bread;
But when she came back
The poor dog was dead.

She went to the undertaker's
To buy him a coffin;
But when she came back
The poor dog was laughing.

She took a clean dish
To get him some tripe;
But when she came back
He was smoking a pipe.

She went to the fishmonger's
To buy him some fish;
But when she came back
He was licking the dish.

She went to the tavern
For white wine and red;
But when she came back
The dog stood on his head.

She went to the fruiterer's
To buy him some fruit;
But when she came back
He was playing the flute.

She went to the tailor's
To buy him a coat;
But when she came back
He was riding a goat.

She went to the hatter's
To buy him a hat;
But when she came back
He was feeding the cat.

She went to the barber's
To buy him a wig;
But when she came back
He was dancing a jig.

She went to the cobbler's
To buy him some shoes;
But when she came back
He was reading the news.

She went to the seamstress
To buy him some linen;
But when she came back
The dog was a-spinning.

She went to the hosier's
To buy him some hose;
But when she came back
He was dressed in his clothes.

The dame made a curtsey,
The dog made a bow;
The dame said, "Your servant",
The dog said, "Bow-wow".

TOMMY TUCKER

*Although not usually sung as a round, this tune will in fact work as such. The asterisk shows the entry-point of the 2nd. voice.

Tommy Tucker

Little Tommy Tucker
Sings for his supper:
What shall we give him?
White bread and butter.
How shall he cut it
Without e'er a knife?
How will he be married
Without e'er a wife?

RIDE A COCK-HORSE

Ride a cock-horse

Ride a cock-horse to Banbury Cross,
To see a fine lady upon a white horse;
Rings on her fingers, and bells on her toes,
She shall have music wherever she goes.

THERE WAS A CROOKED MAN

There was a crooked man

There was a crooked man,
And he walked a crooked mile,
He found a crooked sixpence
Against a crooked stile.
He bought a crooked cat,
Which caught a crooked mouse,
And they all lived together
In a little crooked house.

BOBBY SHAFTO

Fairly fast

1. Bob - by Shaf - to's gone to sea, ___ Sil - ver buck - les
at his knee; ___ He'll come back and mar - ry me, ___
Bon - ny Bob - by Shaf - to! Bob - by Shaf-to's bright and fair,
Comb - ing down his yel - low hair; He's my love for

*If desired, the L.H. chords may be spread throughout in imitation of a guitar.

Bobby Shafto

Bobby Shafto's gone to sea,
Silver buckles at his knee;
He'll come back and marry me,
Bonny Bobby Shafto!
Bobby Shafto's bright and fair,
Combing down his yellow hair;
He's my love for evermore,
Bonny Bobby Shafto!

Bobby Shafto's tall and slim,
He's always dressed so neat and trim;
The ladies they all keek at him,
Bonny Bobby Shafto!
Bobby Shafto's getten a bairn,
For to dandle in his arm;
In his arm and on his knee,
Bobby Shafto loves me!

GOOSEY, GOOSEY GANDER

Humorously

SPOKEN

Gob - ble, gob - ble!   Gob - ble, gob - ble!

Goos - ey, goos - ey gan - der, Whi - ther shall I wan - der?

Up - stairs and down - stairs And in my la - dy's cham - ber.

There I met an old man Who would not say his prayers, I

took him by the left leg And threw him down the stairs.

SPOKEN

Gob - ble, gob - ble!   Gob - ble, gob - ble!

Goosey, goosey gander

Goosey, goosey gander,
Whither shall I wander?
Upstairs and downstairs
And in my lady's chamber.
There I met an old man
Who would not say his prayers,
I took him by the left leg
And threw him down the stairs.

33

Slowly and gently

1. Gold - en slum - bers kiss your eyes, Smiles a -
- wake you when you rise: Sleep, pret - ty wan - tons,
do_ not cry,_ And I will sing a lul - la -
- by.

Golden slumbers

Golden slumbers kiss your eyes,
Smiles awake you when you rise:
Sleep, pretty wantons, do not cry,
And I will sing a lullaby.

Care you know not, therefore sleep,
While over you our watch we keep;
Sleep, pretty darlings, do not cry,
And I will sing a lullaby.

PERC. or SPOKEN

Wea - sel!

Pop! goes the weasel

Up and down the City Road,
In and out the Eagle,
That's the way the money goes,
Pop! goes the weasel.
Half a pound of tuppenny rice,
Half a pound of treacle,
Mix it up and make it nice,
Pop! goes the weasel.

ONE, TWO, BUCKLE MY SHOE

One, Two, Buckle my shoe

1, 2, Buckle my shoe,
3, 4, Knock at the door,
5, 6, Pick up sticks,
7, 8, Lay them straight,
9, 10, A big fat hen,
11, 12, Dig and delve,
13, 14, Maids a-courting,
15, 16, Maids in the kitchen,
17, 18, Maids in waiting,
19, 20, My plate's empty!

HOW DOES MY LADY'S GARDEN GROW?

How does my lady's garden grow?
How does my lady's garden grow?
With silver bells and cockle shells,
And pretty maids all in a row.

Ring-a-ring o' roses,
A pocket full of posies;
One for you, and one for me,
And one for little Moses— } *optional*
Hush-a, Hush-a, we all fall down.

THE MUFFIN MAN

The Muffin Man

O, have you seen the Muffin Man,
The Muffin Man, the Muffin Man:
O, have you seen the Muffin Man,
That lives in Drury Lane?

O yes, I've seen the Muffin Man,
The Muffin Man, the Muffin Man:
O yes, I've seen the Muffin Man,
That lives in Drury Lane.

LITTLE POLLY FLINDERS

Little Polly Flinders Sat a-mong the cin-ders,

Warm-ing her pret-ty lit-tle toes; Her

mo-ther came and caught her, And whipped her lit-tle daugh-ter For

spoil-ing her nice new clothes.

Little Polly Flinders

Little Polly Flinders
Sat among the cinders,
Warming her pretty little toes;
Her mother came and caught her,
And whipped her little daughter
For spoiling her nice new clothes.

With a swing

Up-on Paul's steeple stands a tree, As full of ap-ples as may be; The lit-tle boys of Lon-don town They run with hooks to pull them down: And then they run from hedge to hedge, Un-

46

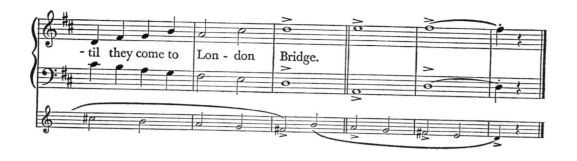

til they come to Lon - don Bridge.

Paul's steeple

Upon Paul's steeple stands a tree,
As full of apples as may be;
The little boys of London town
They run with hooks to pull them down:
And then they run from hedge to hedge,
Until they come to London Bridge.

THIS PIG WENT TO MARKET

This pig went to market

This pig went to market,
This pig stayed at home,
This pig had a bit of meat
And this pig had none;
This pig said—"Wee! wee! wee!
I can't find my way home!"

O DEAR, WHAT CAN THE MATTER BE?

Rather fast

O dear, what can the mat-ter be? Dear, dear, what can the mat-ter be? O dear, what can the mat-ter be?

(End here)

John-ny's so long at the fair._____ 1. He pro-mised he'd buy me a fair-ing should please me, And then for a kiss, Oh! he

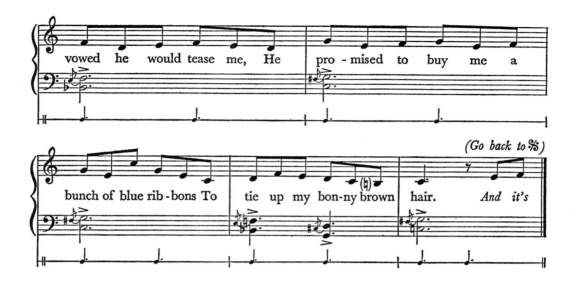

(Go back to %)

O dear, what can the matter be?

O dear, what can the matter be?
Dear, dear, what can the matter be?
O dear, what can the matter be?
Johnny's so long at the fair.

He promised he'd buy me a fairing should please me,
And then for a kiss, Oh! he vowed he would tease me,
He promised he'd bring me a bunch of blue ribbons
To tie up my bonny brown hair.
And it's . . .

He promised he'd bring me a basket of posies,
A garland of lilies, a garland of roses,
A little straw hat, to set off the blue ribbons
That tie up my bonny brown hair.
And it's . . .

THREE BLIND MICE*

*This song may also be sung as a round for 3 voices, as indicated.

52

Three blind mice

Three blind mice,
Three blind mice,
See how they run,
See how they run:
They all ran after the farmer's wife,
Who cut off their tails with a carving knife,
Did ever you see such a thing in your life,
As three blind mice?

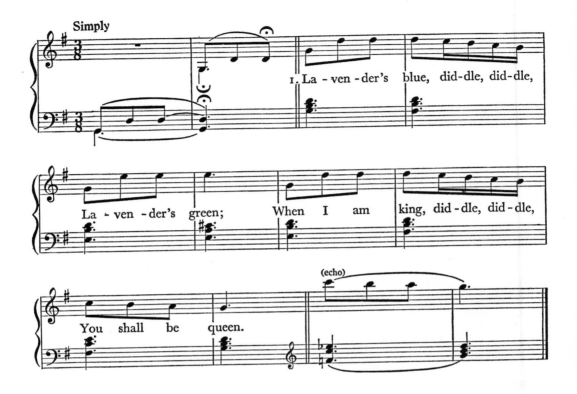

Lavender's blue, diddle, diddle,
Lavender's green;
When I am king, diddle, diddle,
You shall be queen.

Who told you so, diddle, diddle,
Who told you so?
'Twas mine own heart, diddle, diddle,
That told me so.

Call up your men, diddle, diddle,
Set them to work,
Some to the plough, diddle, diddle,
Some to the fork.

Some to make hay, diddle, diddle,
Some to reap corn,
Whilst you and I, diddle, diddle,
Keep the bed warm.

Roses are red, diddle, diddle,
Violets are blue;
Because you love me, diddle, diddle,
I will love you.

Let the birds sing, diddle, diddle,
And the lambs play;
We shall be safe, diddle, diddle,
Out of harm's way.

LITTLE BOY BLUE

Lit - tle Boy Blue, come blow__ your horn, The sheep's in the mea-dow, the cow's in the corn. Where is the boy who looks af - ter the sheep? He's un-der a hay - cock, fast a - sleep. Will you wake him? No, not I, For if I do,__ he's sure to cry.

Little Boy Blue

Little Boy Blue, come blow your horn,
The sheep's in the meadow, the cow's in the corn.
Where is the boy who looks after the sheep?
He's under a haycock, fast asleep.
Will you wake him? No, not I,
For if I do, he's sure to cry.

MARY HAD A LITTLE LAMB

Mary had a little lamb

Mary had a little lamb,
Its fleece was white as snow;
And everywhere that Mary went
The lamb was sure to go.
It followed her to school one day,
That was against the rule;
It made the children laugh and play
To see a lamb at school.

And so the teacher turned it out,
But still it lingered near,
And waited patiently about
Till Mary did appear.
"Why does the lamb love Mary so?"
The eager children cry;
"Why, Mary loves the lamb, you know,"
The teacher did reply.

GIRLS AND BOYS COME OUT TO PLAY

Fairly fast

1. Girls and boys come out to play, The moon doth shine as bright as day. Leave your sup-per and leave your sleep, And join your play-fel-lows in the street.

*For variety, the class may be divided into the two sexes, with the girls starting off alone and the boys joining in at this point.

Girls and boys come out to play

Girls and boys come out to play,
The moon doth shine as bright as day.
Leave your supper and leave your sleep,
And join your playfellows in the street.

Come with a whoop, and come with a call,
Come with a good will or not at all.
Up the ladder and down the wall,
A half-penny loaf will serve us all.

Spoken:
You find milk, and I'll find flour,
And we'll have a pudding in half an hour.

1. Tom, he was a pi-per's son, He learnt to play when he was young, And all the tune that he could play Was, "O-ver the hills and far a-way". O-ver the hills and a great way off, The wind shall blow my top-knot off.

Over the Hills and Far Away

Tom, he was a piper's son,
He learnt to play when he was young,
And all the tune that he could play
Was, "Over the hills and far away".
Over the hills and a great way off,
The wind shall blow my top-knot off.

Tom with his pipe made such a noise,
That he pleased both the girls and boys;
And they all stopped to hear him play,
"Over the hills and far away".
Over the hills, etc.

Tom with his pipe did play with such skill
That those who heard him could never keep still;
As soon as he played they began for to dance,
Even pigs on their hind legs would after him prance.
Over the hills, etc.

As Dolly was milking her cow one day,
Tom took his pipe and began for to play;
So Doll and the cow danced "The Cheshire Round",
Till the pail was broken and the milk ran on the ground.
Over the hills, etc.

He met old Dame Trot with a basket of eggs,
He used his pipe and she used her legs;
She danced about till the eggs were all broke,
She began for to fret, but he laughed at the joke.
Over the hills, etc.

Tom saw a cross fellow was beating an ass,
Heavy laden with pots, pans, dishes, and glass;
He took out his pipe and he played them a tune,
And the poor donkey's load was lightened full soon.
Over the hills, etc.

HOT CROSS BUNS!

*The first 4 bars of this tune may be sung as a round. The asterisk shows the entry-point of the 2nd. voice.

Hot cross buns!

Hot cross buns! Hot cross buns!
One a penny, two a penny, hot cross buns!
If you have no daughters, give them to your sons,
One a penny, two a penny, hot cross buns!

The hart he loves the high wood,
The hare she loves the hill;
The knight he loves his bright sword,
The lady loves her will.

*Although not usually sung as a round, this tune will in fact work as such. The asterisk shows the entry-point of the 2nd. voice.

HEY DIDDLE, DIDDLE

Hey diddle, diddle, the cat and the fiddle,
The cow jumped over the moon;
The little dog laughed to see such sport,
And the dish ran away with the spoon.

HICKORY, DICKORY, DOCK

*Although not usually sung as a round, this tune will in fact work as such. The asterisk shows the entry-point of the 2nd. voice.

Hickory, dickory, dock

Tick tock! Tick tock! Tick tock! Tick tock!
Hickory, dickory, dock,
The mouse ran up the clock.
The clock struck one,
The mouse ran down,
Hickory, dickory, dock.
Hickory, dickory, dock.
Tick tock! Tick tock! Tick tock! Tick tock!

This Old Man

This old man, he played one,
He played nick nack on my drum;
Nick nack paddy whack, give a dog a bone,
This old man came rolling home.

This old man, he played two,
He played nick nack on my shoe;
Nick nack paddy whack, give a dog a bone,
This old man came rolling home.

This old man, he played three,
He played nick nack on my tree;
Nick nack, etc.

This old man, he played four,
He played nick nack on my door;
Nick nack, etc.

This old man, he played five,
He played nick nack on my hive;
Nick nack, etc.

This old man, he played six,
He played nick nack on my sticks;
Nick nack, etc.

This old man, he played seven,
He played nick nack all round Heaven;
Nick nack, etc.

This old man, he played eight,
He played nick nack on my gate;
Nick nack, etc.

This old man, he played nine,
He played nick nack on my line;
Nick nack, etc.

This old man, he played ten,
He played nick nack on my hen;
Nick nack, etc.

MISTRESS BOND

Moderate tempo

SPOKEN

Quack! Quack! Quack! Quack! Quack! Quack!

1. "Oh,— what have you got for din-ner, Mis-tress Bond?" "There's beef— in the lar - der and ducks in the pond"; Dil - ly, dil - ly, dil - ly, dil - ly, come— to be killed; For you— must be stuffed and my cus - to-mers filled!

Mistress Bond

"Oh, what have you got for dinner, Mistress Bond?"
"There's beef in the larder, and ducks in the pond";
Dilly, dilly, dilly, dilly, come to be killed,
For you must be stuffed and my customers filled!

"Send us the beef in, good Mistress Bond,
And get us some ducks dressed out of the pond."
Dilly, dilly, etc.

"John Ostler, go fetch me a duckling or two!"
"Madam," says John Ostler, "I'll try what I can do."
Dilly, dilly, etc.

"I have been to the ducks that swim in the pond,
But I found they will not come to be killed, Mistress Bond."
Dilly, dilly, etc.

Mistress Bond she flew down to the pond in a rage,
With plenty of onions and plenty of sage.
Dilly, dilly, etc.

She cried, "Little wag-tails, come and be killed,
For you must be stuffed and my customers filled!"
Dilly, dilly, etc.

73

Little Miss Muffet

Little Miss Muffet sat on a tuffet,
Eating her curds and whey;
There came a big spider, who sat down beside her
And frightened Miss Muffet away.

Little Jack Horner

Little Jack Horner sat in the corner,
Eating a Christmas pie;
He put in his thumb, and pulled out a plum,
And said, "What a good boy am I!"

THE LADY AND THE SWINE

1. There was a la - dy loved a swine:

SPOKEN
Hunc! Hunc!

"'Ho - ney," said she, "Pig - hog, wilt thou be mine?"

"Hunc," said he.

SPOKEN
Hunc!

*Although not usually sung as a round, this tune will in fact work as such. The asterisk shows the entry-point of the 2nd. voice.

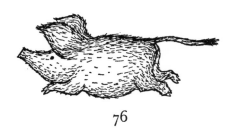

The Lady and the Swine

There was a lady loved a swine:
"Honey," said she,
"Pig-hog, wilt thou be mine?"
"Hunc," said he.

"I'll build for thee a silver sty,
Honey," said she,
"So that in it thou shalt lie,"
"Hunc," said he.

"I'll latch it with a silver pin,
Honey," said she,
"That thou may go out and in."
"Hunc," said he.

"O, wilt thou then have me now,
Honey?" said she,
"Speak, or else my heart will break."
"Hunc," said he.

Fairly fast

Here we go ga - ther-ing nuts in May, nuts in May,
Here we go round the mul - berry bush, The mul - berry bush, the

nuts in May, Here we go ga - ther-ing nuts in May, on a
mul - berry bush: Here we go round the mul - berry bush, On a

cold and fros - ty morn - ing.
cold and fros - ty morn - ing.

The Mulberry Bush

Here we go round the mulberry bush,
The mulberry bush, the mulberry bush:
Here we go round the mulberry bush,
On a cold and frosty morning.

This is the way we wash our hands,
Wash our hands, wash our hands:
This is the way we wash our hands,
On a cold and frosty morning.

Here we go round the mulberry bush, etc.

This is the way we wash our clothes, etc.

Here we go round the mulberry bush, etc.

This is the way we dry our clothes, etc.

Here we go round the mulberry bush, etc.

This is the way we iron our clothes, etc.

Here we go round the mulberry bush, etc.

This is the way we sweep the floor, etc.

Here we go round the mulberry bush, etc.

This is the way we brush our hair, etc.

Here we go round the mulberry bush, etc.

This is the way we clean our boots, etc.

Here we go round the mulberry bush, etc.

This is the way we make the bread, etc.

Here we go round the mulberry bush, etc.

This is the way we clean our rooms, etc.

Here we go round the mulberry bush, etc.

This is the way we go to school, etc.

Here we go round the mulberry bush, etc.

This is the way we come back from school, etc.

Here we go round the mulberry bush, etc.

Nuts in May

Here we go gathering nuts in May, nuts in May, nuts in May,
Here we go gathering nuts in May, on a cold and frosty morning.

Pat-a-cake

Pat-a-cake, pat-a-cake, baker's man,
Bake me a cake as fast as you can.
Pat it and prick it, and mark it with B,
Put it in the oven for Baby and me.

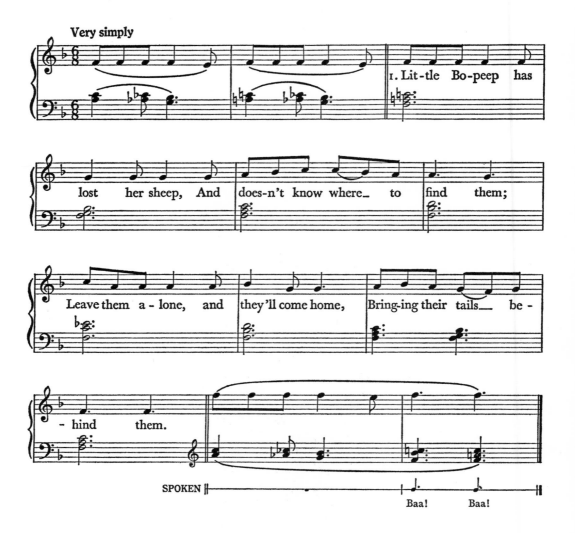

Little Bo-peep

Little Bo-peep has lost her sheep,
And doesn't know where to find them;
Leave them alone, and they'll come home,
Bringing their tails behind them.

Little Bo-peep fell fast asleep,
And dreamt she heard them bleating;
But when she awoke, she found it a joke,
For they were still a-fleeting.

Then up she took her little crook,
Determined for to find them;
She'd found them indeed, but it made her heart bleed,
For they'd left their tails behind them.

It happened one day, as Bo-peep did stray
Into a meadow hard by,
There she espied their tails side by side,
All hung on a tree to dry.

She heaved a sigh, and wiped her eye,
And over the hillocks went rambling,
And tried what she could, as a shepherdess should,
To tack again each to its lambkin.

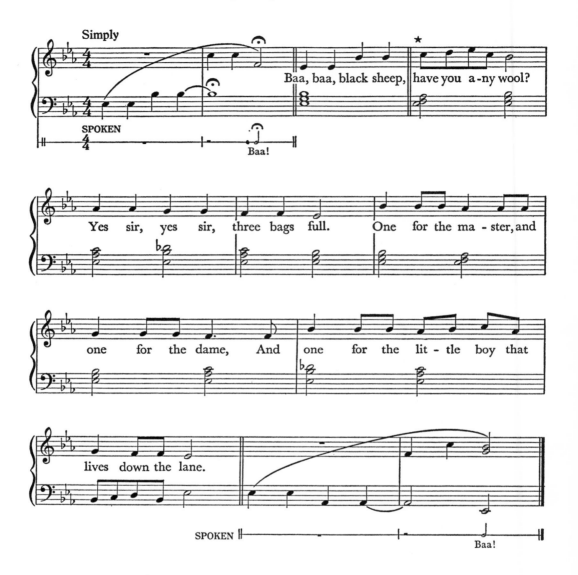

Baa, baa, black sheep, have you any wool?
Yes sir, yes sir, three bags full.
One for the master, and one for the dame,
And one for the little boy that lives down the lane.

*Although not usually sung as a round, this tune will in fact work as such. The asterisk shows the entry-point of the 2nd. voice.

Hush-a-bye, baby, on the tree top:
When the wind blows the cradle will rock;
When the bough breaks the cradle will fall,
Down will come baby, cradle, and all!

★These words may also be sung to the tune of *Lilliburlero* (1st. half). Minor adjustments to the L.H.
accompaniment are necessary if this is done. (See *The Old Woman tossed up in a Basket*, p. 154.)

I LOVE LITTLE PUSSY

*Although not usually sung as a round, this tune will in fact work as such. The asterisk shows the entry-point of the 2nd. voice.

I love little pussy

I love little pussy,
Her coat is so warm;
And if I don't hurt her,
She'll do me no harm.

So I'll not pull her tail,
Nor drive her away;
But pussy and I
Very gently will play.

She will sit by my side,
And I'll give her some food;
And pussy will love me
Because I am good.

The north wind doth blow,
And we shall have snow,
And what will poor Robin do then, poor thing?
He'll sit in a barn,
And keep himself warm,
And hide his head under his wing, poor thing!

LADYBIRD, LADYBIRD

Ladybird, ladybird, fly away home!
Your house is on fire, and your children all gone;
All except one and that's little Ann
And she has crept under the warming pan.

PEASE PUDDING HOT

*Although not usually sung as a round, this tune will in fact work as such. The asterisk shows the entry-point of the 2nd. voice.

Pease pudding hot

Pease pudding hot, pease pudding cold.
Pease pudding in the pot, nine days old.
Some like it hot, some like it cold,
Some like it in the pot, nine days old.

THE LITTLE NUT TREE

1. I had a lit-tle nut tree: no-thing would it bear, But a sil-ver nut-meg and a gold-en pear. The King of Spain's daugh-ter came to vi-sit me, And all for the sake of my lit-tle nut tree.

The Little Nut Tree

I had a little nut tree: nothing would it bear,
But a silver nutmeg and a golden pear.
The King of Spain's daughter came to visit me,
And all for the sake of my little nut tree.

I had a little nut tree: nothing would it bear,
But a silver nutmeg and a golden pear.
I skipped over water, I danced over sea,
And all the birds in the air couldn't catch me.

ORANGES AND LEMONS

*Any one of the percussion figures A, B and C may be used from the 1st. double barline to the 12/8, if a more simple part is required.

-ditch. Pray, when will that be? Say the bells of Step -

- ney. I'm sure I don't know, Says the great bell at

Bow. Here comes a can-dle to light you to bed, Here

comes a chop-per to chop off your head. The last, last, last, ...

SPOKEN: .... last man's head.

95

Oranges and Lemons

Oranges and lemons,
Say the bells of St. Clement's,
You owe me five farthings,
Say the bells of St. Martin's.
When will you pay me?
Say the bells of Old Bailey.
When I grow rich,
Say the bells of Shoreditch.
Pray, when will that be?
Say the bells of Stepney.
I'm sure I don't know,
Says the great bell at Bow.
Here comes a candle to light you to bed,
Here comes a chopper to chop off your head.
The last, last, last, . . . làst man's head.

Gay go up and gay go down,
To ring the bells of London town.
Bull's eyes and targets,
Say the bells of St. Marg'ret's.
Brickbats and tiles,
Say the bells of St. Giles'.
Pancakes and fritters,
Say the bells of St. Peter's.
Two sticks and an apple,
Say the bells at Whitechapel.
Old Father Baldpate,
Say the slow bells at Aldgate.

Maids in white aprons,
Say the bells at St. Catherine's.
Pokers and tongs,
Say the bells at St. John's.
Kettles and pans,
Say the bells at St. Anne's.
When will you pay me?
Say the bells at Old Bailey.
When I grow rich,
Say the bells at Shoreditch.
Pray, when will that be?
Say the bells at Stepney.
I'm sure I don't know,
Says the great bell at Bow.

O, DEAR SIXPENCE!

O, dear sixpence!
I love sixpence!
I love sixpence as I love my life;
I'll spend a penny on't,
I'll lend another on't,
And I'll carry fourpence home to my wife.

London Bridge

1. London Bridge is broken down,
   Broken down, broken down,
   London Bridge is broken down,
   My fair lady.

2. Build it up with wood and clay, etc.
3. Wood and clay will wash away, etc.
4. Build it up with bricks and mortar, etc.
5. Bricks and mortar will not stay, etc.
6. Build it up with iron and steel, etc.
7. Iron and steel will bend and bow, etc.
8. Build it up with silver and gold, etc.
9. Silver and gold will be stolen away, etc.
10. Set a man to watch all night, etc.
11. Suppose the man should fall asleep, etc.
12. Give him a pipe to smoke all night, etc.

TOM, TOM, THE PIPER'S SON

Tom, Tom, the pi-per's son, Stole a pig and a-way he run. The pig was eat, and Tom was beat, And Tom went howl-ing down the street.

Tom, Tom, the piper's son

Tom, Tom, the piper's son,
Stole a pig and away he run.
The pig was eat, and Tom was beat,
And Tom went howling down the street.

WHAT ARE LITTLE BOYS MADE OF?★

★For variety, the class may be divided into the two sexes, each group singing the description of the other group's sex. Alternatively, the two groups could sing the sung and the spoken parts respectively.

†The spoken parts are optional.

What are little boys made of?

What are little boys made of, made of?
What are little boys made of?
Frogs and snails and puppy-dogs' tails,
And such are little boys made of.

Frogs and snails and puppy-dogs' tails,
And such are little boys made of.

What are little girls made of, made of?
What are little girls made of?
Sugar and spice and all things nice,
And such are little girls made of.

Sugar and spice and all things nice,
And such are little girls made of.

What are our young men made of, made of?
What are our young men made of?
Sighs and leers and crocodile tears,
And such are our young men made of.

Sighs and leers and crocodile tears,
And such are our young men made of.

What are our young women made of, made of?
What are our young women made of?
Ribbons and laces and sweet pretty faces,
And such are young women made of.

Ribbons and laces and sweet pretty faces,
And such are young women made of.

Humpty Dumpty

Humpty Dumpty sat on a wall,
Humpty Dumpty had a great fall:
All the King's horses and all the King's men,
Couldn't put Humpty together again.

CURLY LOCKS!

Cur-ly locks! Cur-ly locks! wilt thou be mine?— Thou shalt not wash di-shes, nor yet feed the swine; But sit on a cu-shion and sew a fine seam,— And feed up-on straw-ber-ries, su-gar and cream.

Curly Locks!

Curly locks! Curly locks! wilt thou be mine?
Thou shalt not wash dishes, nor yet feed the swine;
But sit on a cushion and sew a fine seam,
And feed upon strawberries, sugar and cream.

Twinkle, twinkle, little star

Twinkle, twinkle, little star,
How I wonder what you are!
Up above the world so high,
Like a diamond in the sky.
Twinkle, twinkle, little star,
How I wonder what you are!

When the blazing sun is gone,
When he nothing shines upon,
Then you show your little light,
Twinkle, twinkle, all the night.
Twinkle, etc.

Then the traveller in the dark
Thanks you for your tiny spark,
He could not see which way to go
If you did not twinkle so.
Twinkle, etc.

In the dark blue sky you keep,
And often through my curtains peep,
For you never shut your eye
'Till the sun is in the sky.
Twinkle, etc.

As your bright and tiny spark,
Lights one traveller in the dark,
Though I know not what you are,
Twinkle, twinkle, little star.

Pussy cat, pussy cat

Pussy cat, pussy cat, where have you been?
"I've been to London to look at the Queen."
Pussy cat, pussy cat, what did you there?
"I frightened a little mouse under her chair."

The Man with the Gun

There was a little man,
And he had a little gun,
And his bullets were made of lead, lead, lead.
He went to the brook,
And he shot a little duck,
Right through the middle of the head, head, head.

And then he took it home
To his little wife Joan,
And bade her a fire for to make, make, make,
To roast the little duck
He had shot in the brook,
While he went to look for the drake, drake, drake.

The drake he was a-swimming
With his little curly tail,
The little man made it his mark, mark, mark.
He let off his gun,
But he fired too soon,
And the drake flew away with a quack, quack, quack.

One, two, three, four, five,
Once I caught a fish a - live;
Why did you let it go? Be - cause it bit my fin - ger so.

Six, sev'n, eight, nine, ten,
Then I let it go a - gain.
Which fin - ger did it bite? This lit - tle fin - ger on the right.

One, two, three, four, five

One, two, three, four, five,
Once I caught a fish alive;
Six, seven, eight, nine, ten,
Then I let it go again.

Why did you let it go?
Because it bit my finger so.
Which finger did it bite?
This little finger on the right.

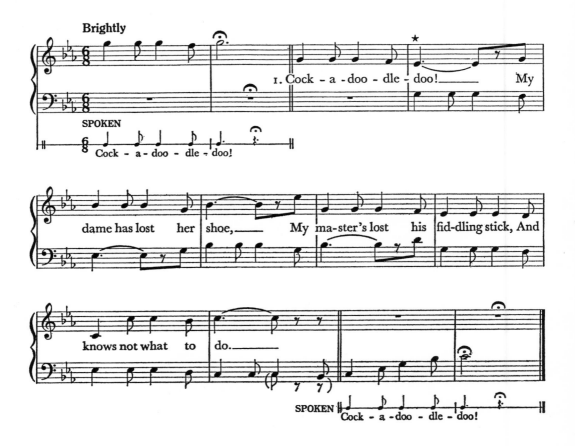

*Although not usually sung as a round, this tune will in fact work as such with the single note alteration in bar 4 of the tune (bar 5, piano L.H.). The asterisk shows the entry-point of the 2nd. voice.

Cock-a-doodle-doo!

Cock-a-doodle-doo!
My dame has lost her shoe,
My master's lost his fiddling stick,
And knows not what to do.

Cock-a-doodle-doo!
What is my dame to do?
Till master finds his fiddling stick
She'll dance without her shoe.

Cock-a-doodle-doo!
My dame has found her shoe,
And master's found his fiddling stick,
Sing doodle-doodle-doo.

Cock-a-doodle-doo!
My dame will dance with you,
While master fiddles his fiddling stick
For dame and doodle-doo.

WHERE ARE YOU GOING TO, MY PRETTY MAID?

1. Where are you go-ing to, my pret-ty maid? Where are you go-ing to, my pret-ty maid? I'm go-ing a-milk-ing, sir, she said, Sir, she said, sir, she said, I'm go-ing a-milk-ing, sir, she said.

Where are you going to, my pretty maid?

Where are you going to, my pretty maid?
I'm going a-milking, sir, she said,
Sir, she said, sir, she said,
I'm going a-milking, sir, she said.

May I go with you, my pretty maid?
You're kindly welcome, sir, she said,
Sir, she said, sir, she said,
You're kindly welcome, sir, she said.

Say, will you marry me, my pretty maid?
Yes, if you please, kind sir, she said,
Sir, she said, sir, she said,
Yes, if you please, kind sir, she said.

What is your father, my pretty maid?
My father's a farmer, sir, she said,
Sir, she said, sir, she said,
My father's a farmer, sir, she said.

What is your fortune, my pretty maid?
My face is my fortune, sir, she said,
Sir, she said, sir, she said,
My face is my fortune, sir, she said.

Then I can't marry you, my pretty maid.
Nobody asked you, sir, she said,
Sir, she said, sir, she said,
Nobody asked you, sir, she said.

THERE WAS AN OLD WOMAN

Rather sadly

There was an old wo-man who lived — in a shoe, She had so ma-ny chil-dren she did-n't know what to do; She gave them some broth with-out a-ny bread; She whipped them all sound-ly and sent — them to bed.

There was an old woman who lived in a shoe

There was an old woman who lived in a shoe,
She had so many children she didn't know what to do;
She gave them some broth without any bread;
She whipped them all soundly and sent them to bed.

Sing a song of sixpence

Sing a song of sixpence,
A pocket full of rye;
Four-and-twenty blackbirds
Baked in a pie.
When the pie was opened,
The birds began to sing;
Was not that a dainty dish
To set before the king?

The king was in his counting-house,
Counting out his money;
The queen was in the parlour,
Eating bread and honey.
The maid was in the garden,
Hanging out the clothes,
When down came a blackbird
And pecked off her nose.

Rather fast

Green gra-vel, green gra-vel, your grass is so green — The fair-est young dam-sel that e-ver was seen. We washed her, we dried her, we clothed her in silk, And we wrote down her name with a

(sustain)

(let ring)

gold pen and ink. O An - nie, O An - nie, your true love is dead, And we send you a let - ter to turn round your head.

Green Gravel

Green gravel, green gravel, your grass is so green—
The fairest young damsel that ever was seen.
We washed her, we dried her, we clothed her in silk,
And we wrote down her name with a gold pen and ink.
O Annie, O Annie, your true love is dead,
And we send you a letter to turn round your head.

DOCTOR FOSTER

Doctor Foster

Doctor Foster went to Gloucester
In a shower of rain;
He slipped in a puddle, right up to his middle,
And never went there again!

Gaily—and a little bizarre!

1. If all the world were pa - per, And all the sea were ink,— If all the trees were bread and cheese, What should we have to drink?

If all the world were paper

If all the world were paper,
And all the sea were ink,
If all the trees were bread and cheese,
What should we have to drink?

If all the world were sand-o,
Oh then what should we lack-o?
If as they say there were no clay,
How should we take tobacco?

If all things were eternal,
And nothing their end bringing,
If this should be, then how should we,
Here make an end of singing?

la - dle, And his name was Ai - ken Drum.

Aiken Drum

There was a man lived in the moon,
And his name was Aiken Drum;
And he played upon a ladle,
And his name was Aiken Drum.

And his hat was made of good cream cheese,
And his name was Aiken Drum;
And he played, etc.

And his coat was made of good roast beef,
And his name was Aiken Drum;
And he played, etc.

And his buttons were made of penny loaves,
And his name was Aiken Drum;
And he played, etc.

His waistcoat was made of crust of pies,
And his name was Aiken Drum;
And he played, etc.

His breeches were made of haggis bags,
And his name was Aiken Drum;
And he played, etc.

LAZY SHEEP, PRAY TELL ME WHY

Lazy sheep, pray tell me why

Lazy sheep, pray tell me why
In the pleasant field you lie,
Eating grass and daisies white
From the morning till the night?
Every thing can something do,
But what kind of use are you?

POOR JENNY SITS A-WEEPING

(Back to 𝄋 for vv. 3 & 4)

[Turn to page 136]

134

Poor Jenny sits a-weeping

1. Poor Jenny sits a-weeping,
   A-weeping, a-weeping,
   Poor Jenny sits a-weeping,
   On a bright summer's day.

2. Pray, Jenny, tell me what you're weeping for,
   A-weeping for, a-weeping for:
   Pray, tell me what you're weeping for,
   On a bright summer's day.

3. I'm weeping for a sweetheart, etc.

4. O pray, get up and choose one, etc.

(Turn for v. 5.)

5. Now you're married, we wish you joy,
   First a girl and then a boy;
   Seven years after, son and daughter.
   Pray, young couple, come kiss together.
   Kiss her once, kiss her twice,
   Kiss her three times over.

5. Now you're mar-ried, we wish you joy, First a girl and then a boy; Se-ven years af - ter, son and daugh - ter. Pray, young cou - ple, come kiss to - ge - ther. Kiss her once, kiss her twice, Kiss her three times o - ver.

(damp)

136

HIGGLEDY, PIGGLEDY, MY BLACK HEN

Higgledy, piggledy, my black hen,
She lays eggs for gentlemen.
Sometimes nine and sometimes ten,
Higgledy, piggledy, my black hen.

★ Tap on piano woodwork with R. H.

Rub-a-dub-dub

Rub-a-dub-dub,
Three men in a tub,
And who do you think they be?
The butcher, the baker, the candlestick-maker,
Turn 'em out
Knaves all three!

A FROG HE WOULD A-WOOING GO

A frog he would a-wooing go

A frog he would a-wooing go,
Heigh ho! says Rowley,
Whether his mother would let him or no.
With a rowley, powley, gammon and spinach,
Heigh ho! says Anthony Rowley.

So off he set with his opera hat,
Heigh ho!, etc.
And on the road he met with a rat.
With a rowley, powley, etc.

Pray, Mister Rat, will you go with me?
Kind Mistress Mousey for to see?

They came to the door of Mousey's hall,
They gave a loud knock, and they gave a loud call.

Pray, Mistress Mouse, are you within?
Oh yes, kind sirs, I'm sitting to spin.

Pray, Mistress Mouse, will you give us some beer?
For Froggy and I are fond of good cheer.

Pray, Mister Frog, will you give us a song?
Let it be something that's not very long.

Indeed, Mistress Mouse, replied Mister Frog,
A cold has made me as hoarse as a dog.

Since you have a cold, Mister Frog, Mousey said,
I'll sing you a song that I have just made.

But while they were all a-merry-making,
A cat and her kittens came tumbling in.

The cat she seized the rat by the crown,
The kittens they pulled the little mouse down.

This put Mister Frog in a terrible fright,
He took up his hat and he wished them good-night.

But as Froggy was crossing over a brook,
A lily-white duck came and gobbled him up.

So there was an end of one, two, three,
The rat, the mouse, and the little frog-ee.

OLD KING COLE

Moderate tempo

Old King Cole was a mer-ry old soul, And a mer-ry old soul was he; He called for his pipe, And he called for his bowl, And he called for his fid - dlers three. Ev - 'ry fid-dler he had a fid-dle, And a ve-ry fine fid-dle had he; Oh, there's none so rare As can com-pare With King Cole and his fid - dlers three.

Old King Cole

Old King Cole was a merry old soul,
And a merry old soul was he;
He called for his pipe,
And he called for his bowl,
And he called for his fiddlers three.
Every fiddler, he had a fiddle,
And a very fine fiddle had he;
Oh, there's none so rare
As can compare
With King Cole and his fiddlers three.

THREE MICE WENT INTO A HOLE TO SPIN

Not too fast

1. Three

mice went in-to a hole to spin; Puss passed by, and Puss peeped in.

"What are you do-ing, my lit - tle men?" "Weav-ing coats_ for

gen - tle-men." "Please let me help you to wind off your threads." "No,

no, Mis - tress Pus - sy, you'd bite off our heads! No,

no, Mis - tress Pus - sy, you'd bite off our heads!"

*Although not usually sung as a round, this tune will in fact work as such. The asterisk shows the **entry-point** of the 2nd. voice.

Three mice went into a hole to spin

Three mice went into a hole to spin;
Puss passed by, and Puss peeped in.
"What are you doing, my little men?"
"Weaving coats for gentlemen."
"Please let me help you to wind off your threads."
"No, no, Mistress Pussy, you'd bite off our heads!
No, no, Mistress Pussy, you'd bite off our heads!"

Says Puss: "You look so wondrous wise,
I like your whiskers and bright black eyes;
Your house is the nicest house I see,
I think there is room for you and me."
The mice were so pleased that they opened the door,
And Pussy soon laid them all dead on the floor,
And Pussy soon laid them all dead on the floor.

WEE WILLIE WINKIE

Wee Willie Winkie

Wee Willie Winkie runs through the town,
Upstairs and downstairs in his night-gown,
Rapping at the window, crying through the lock,
"Are the children all in bed, for it's now eight o'clock?"

A LITTLE COCK-SPARROW

Very simply

SPOKEN

1. A lit - tle cock-spar-row sat

Cheep! Cheep!

on a green tree, And he chir - ruped, he chir - ruped, so

mer - ry was he; A naugh - ty boy came with his

wee bow and ar - row, Says he, "I will shoot this

lit - tle cock-spar-row."(7)

SPOKEN

Cheep! Cheep!

A Little Cock-sparrow

A little cock-sparrow sat on a green tree,
And he chirruped, he chirruped, so merry was he;
A naughty boy came with his wee bow and arrow,
Says he, "I will shoot this little cock-sparrow."

"His body will make me a nice little stew
And his giblets will make me a little pie too."
"Oh, no!", said the sparrow, "I won't make a stew,"
So he clapped his wings and away he flew.

*Although not usually sung as a round, this tune will in fact work as such. The asterisk shows the entry-point of the 2nd. voice.

†For variety, the next 3 bars may be sung in the minor mode.

Billy Pringle

Billy Pringle had a little pig,
When it was young it was not very big,
When it was old it lived in clover,
Now it's dead and that's all over.
Billy Pringle he lay down and died,
Betty Pringle she lay down and cried,
So there was an end of one, two and three,
Billy Pringle he,
Betty Pringle she, and the piggy wiggy wee.

GEORGIE PORGIE

Geor - gie Por - gie, pud-ding and pie, Kissed the girls and made__ them cry; When the boys came out to play, Geor - gie Por - gie ran__ a - way.

Georgie Porgie

Georgie Porgie, pudding and pie,
Kissed the girls and made them cry;
When the boys came out to play,
Georgie Porgie ran away.

THE OLD WOMAN TOSSED UP IN A BASKET*

With a lilt

There was an old wo-man tossed
up in a bask - et, Se - ven - teen times as
high as the moon; Where she was go - ing I
could - n't but ask it, For in her hand she
car - ried a broom. "Old wo - man, old wo - man, old

(sustain)
(let ring)

*See *Hush-a-bye, baby*, p.85.

154

woman," quoth I, "Where are you go - ing to up __ so high?" "To brush __ the cob - webs off __ the sky!" __ "May I __ go with you?" "Aye, by - and - by."

There was an old woman tossed up in a basket,
Seventeen times as high as the moon;
Where she was going I couldn't but ask it,
For in her hand she carried a broom.
"Old woman, old woman, old woman," quoth I,
"Where are you going to up so high?"
"To brush the cobwebs off the sky!"
"May I go with you?" "Aye, by-and-by."

Scissors and String

Scissors and string, scissors and string,
When a man's single he lives like a king.
Needles and pins, needles and pins,
When a man marries his trouble begins.

THIS IS THE WAY THE LADIES RIDE

Sedately

This is the way the la - dies ride, Nim, nim, nim, nim.

This is the way the gen-tle-men ride, Trim, trim, trim, trim.

Faster

This is the way the far-mers ride, Trot, trot, trot, trot.

Faster still

This is the way the hunts - men ride, A - gal-lop, a - gal-lop, a - gal - lop, a - gal - lop.

With great uncertainty (slow)

This is the way the plough-boys ride, Hob -ble -dy - gee, hob-ble-dy-gee.

This is the way the ladies ride

This is the way the ladies ride,
    Nim, nim, nim, nim.
This is the way the gentlemen ride,
    Trim, trim, trim, trim.
This is the way the farmers ride,
    Trot, trot, trot, trot.
This is the way the huntsmen ride,
    A-gallop, a-gallop, a-gallop, a-gallop.
This is the way the ploughboys ride,
    Hobble-dy-gee, hobble-dy-gee.

*In v. 5 (only), *Caw* sounds may be used in the absence of any percussion.

The Carrion Crow

A carrion crow sat on an oak,
Derry, derry, derry, deeco:
A carrion crow sat on an oak,
Watching a tailor shape his cloak:
Heigh ho! the carrion crow,
Derry, derry, derry, deeco!

O wife, bring me my old bent bow,
Derry, derry, derry, deeco:
O wife, bring me my old bent bow,
That I may shoot yon carrion crow:
Heigh ho! the carrion crow,
Derry, derry, derry, deeco!

The tailor shot, and missed his mark,
Derry, derry, derry, deeco:
The tailor shot and missed his mark,
And shot his own sow through the heart:
Heigh ho! the carrion crow,
Derry, derry, derry, deeco!

O wife! o wife! some brandy in a spoon,
Derry, derry, derry, deeco:
O wife! bring me some brandy in a spoon,
For our old sow is in a swoon:
Heigh ho! the carrion crow,
Derry, derry, derry, deeco!

The old sow died, and the bell did toll,
Derry, derry, derry, deeco:
The old sow died, and the bell did toll,
And the little pigs prayed for the old sow's soul:
Heigh ho! the carrion crow,
Derry, derry, derry, deeco!

HEY DIDDLE DUMPLING, MY SON JOHN

*Upper 8ve. optional for piano R.H.

Hey diddle dumpling, my son John

Hey diddle dumpling, my son John,
He went to his bed with his stockings on;
One shoe off and the other shoe on,
Hey diddle dumpling, my son John.

THE OLD WOMAN OF NORWICH

yet this old wo - man could ne - ver keep quiet. (7)

★Food!

★Drink!

The Old Woman of Norwich

There was an old woman, and what do you think?
She lived upon nothing but victuals and drink;
Victuals and drink were the chief of her diet,
And yet this old woman could never keep quiet.

★All shout together.

*Bagpipe noises may be made vocally if preferred.

Pussy cat

Pussy-cat high, Pussy-cat low,
Pussy-cat was a fine teazer of tow.

Pussy-cat she came into the barn,
With her bag-pipes under her arm.

And then she told a tale to me,
How Mousey had married a humble bee.

Then was I ever so glad,
That Mousey had married so clever a lad.

THE SPIDER AND THE FLY★

1. "Will you walk in – to my par - lour?" Said a Spi - der to a Fly, " 'Tis the pret - tiest lit - tle par – lour That e - ver you did spy; The__ way in - to my par-lour is up a wind - ing stair, And I have ma – ny

★The words of Lewis Carroll's *The Lobster Quadrille* (from "Alice in Wonderland") may be sung to this tune.

pret – ty things to show you when you're there". "Oh,

no, no!" said the lit – tle Fly, "To ask me is in

vain, For who goes up your wind – ing stair, shall

ne'er come down a – gain".

The Spider and the Fly

"Will you walk into my parlour?"
Said a Spider to a Fly,
" 'Tis the prettiest little parlour
That ever you did spy;
The way into my parlour is up a winding stair,
And I have many pretty things to show you when you're there".
"Oh, no, no!" said the little Fly,
"To ask me is in vain,
For who goes up your winding stair, shall ne'er come down again".

"I'm sure you must be weary, dear! with soaring up so high,
Will you rest upon my little bed?" said the Spider to the Fly;
"There are pretty curtains drawn around, the sheets are fine and thin,
And if you like to rest awhile, I'll snugly tuck you in":
"Oh, no, no!" said the little Fly, "For I have heard it said,
They never, never wake again who sleep upon your bed".

The Spider turned him round about and went into his den,
For well he knew the silly Fly would soon come back again;
So he wove a subtle web in a little corner sly,
And he set his table ready to dine upon the Fly:
Then he came out to his door again and merrily did sing,
"Come hither, hither, pretty Fly with pearl and silver wing".

Alas! alas! how very soon this silly little Fly,
Hearing all these flattering speeches came quickly buzzing by;
With gauzy wing she hung aloft, then near and nearer drew,
Thinking only of her crested head and gold and purple hue:
Thinking only of her brilliant wings, poor silly thing, at last
Up jumped the wicked Spider and fiercely held her fast!

He dragged her up his winding stair into his dismal den,
Within his little parlour, but she ne'er came out again!
And now all you young maidens who may this story hear,
To idle flattering speeches, I pray you, ne'er give ear:
Unto an evil counsellor close heart and ear and eye,
And learn a lesson from the tale of the Spider and the Fly.

"Mary, Mary, quite contrary,
How does your garden grow?"—
"With silver bells and cockle shells,
And pretty maids all in a row."

See-saw, Margery Daw

See-saw, Margery Daw,
Jacky shall have a new master;
Jacky shall have but a penny a day,
Because he can't work any faster.

See-saw, Margery Daw,
Sold her bed and lay upon straw;
Was not she a dirty slut
To sell her bed and lie in the dust.

DING, DONG, BELL

Firmly

Ding, dong, bell, Pus-sy's in the well.

Who put her in? Lit-tle John-ny Green. Who pulled her out?

Lit - tle Tom - my Trout. What a naugh-ty boy was that To try to

drown poor pus - sy cat, Who ne - ver did him a - ny harm, And

*The first 4 bars of this tune may be sung as a round, as shown by the piano L.H., to the words *Ding, dong, bell*. The asterisk shows the entry-point of the 2nd. voice.